Primary Sources of Westward Expansion

Homesteading and Settling the Frontier

Alison Morretta

Fitchburg Public Library
5530 Lacy Road
Fitchburg, WI 53711

Cavendish Square
New York

Published in 2018 by Cavendish Square Publishing, LLC
243 5th Avenue, Suite 136, New York, NY 10016

Copyright © 2018 by Cavendish Square Publishing, LLC

First Edition

No part of this publication may be reproduced, stored in a retrieval system, or transmitted in any form or by any means—electronic, mechanical, photocopying, recording, or otherwise—without the prior permission of the copyright owner. Request for permission should be addressed to Permissions,
Cavendish Square Publishing, 243 5th Avenue, Suite 136, New York, NY 10016.
Tel (877) 980-4450; fax (877) 980-4454.

Website: cavendishsq.com

This publication represents the opinions and views of the author based on his or her personal experience, knowledge, and research. The information in this book serves as a general guide only. The author and publisher have used their best efforts in preparing this book and disclaim liability rising directly or indirectly from the use and application of this book.

CPSIA Compliance Information: Batch #CS16CSQ

All websites were available and accurate when this book was sent to press.

Library of Congress Cataloging-in-Publication Data
Names: Morretta, Alison, author.
Title: Homesteading and settling the frontier / Alison Morretta.
Description: New York : Cavendish Square Publishing, [2018] |
Series: Primary sources of westward expansion series | Includes bibliographical references and index.
Identifiers: LCCN 2016058846 (print) | LCCN 2017000096 (ebook) |
ISBN 9781502626417 (library bound) | ISBN 9781502626370 (E-book)
Subjects: LCSH: Frontier and pioneer life--West (U.S.)--Juvenile literature. |
Pioneers--West (U.S.)--History--19th century--Juvenile literature. |
West (U.S.)--History--1848-1860--Juvenile literature. |
West (U.S.)--History--1860-1890--Juvenile literature. |
United States--Territorial expansion--Juvenile literature.
Classification: LCC F596 .M6848 2018 (print) | LCC F596 (ebook) |
DDC 978/.02--dc23
LC record available at https://lccn.loc.gov/2016058846

Editorial Director: David McNamara
Editor: Fletcher Doyle
Copy Editor: Nathan Heidelberger
Associate Art Director: Amy Greenan
Designer: Raúl Rodriguez
Production Coordinator: Karol Szymczuk
Photo Research: J8 Media

The photographs in this book are used by permission and through the courtesy of: Cover, David F. Barry/NARA/File: Chief Gall-NARA.jpg/Wikimedia Commons/Public Domain; pp. 4, 6, 10, 24, 28-29 MPI/Archive Photos/Getty Images; p. 9 Ann Ronan Pictures/Print Collector/Getty Images; p. 11 Beyond My Ken, own work/File: Second Bank of the United States front.jpg/Wikimedia Commons/CCA-SA 4.0 International; p. 13 P.S. Duval & Co., c1801 Library of Congress Prints and Photographs Division; p. 17 Unknown/File: Stephen Fuller Austin.jpg/Wikimedia Commons/CCA 2.0 Generic; pp.19, 37 Everett Historical/Shutterstock.com; p. 22 Alfred J. Miller/Exploring the West by Hermann J. Viola/File: Green River meeting.jpg /Wikimedia Commons/Public Domain; p. 26 North Wind Picture Archives; p. 30 Karl Bodmer/File: A Stop; Evening Bivouac by Karl Bodmer 1833.jpg/Wikimedia Commons/Public Domain; pp. 33, 53 Bettmann/Getty Images; p. 34 Hulton Archive/Getty Images; p. 36 NARA/File: Freeman homestead-certificate.jpg - Wikimedia Commons/Public Domain; p. 41 (HABS)Library of Congress Prints and Photographs Division/File: Photocopy of Historic Photograph, Photographer and Date Unknown- Early area homestead, Nicodemus Historic Download District, Nicodemus, Graham County, KS HABS KANS,33-NICO,1-6.tif/Wikimedia Commons/Public Domain; p. 43 Author Unknown/NARA/File: Photograph of A Woman with a Hay Stack - NARA - 7829555.jpg /Wikimedia Commons/Public Domain; p. 47 Photographer unknown/http://www.readthespirit.com/explore/ecotheology/index.html?File: 1890s Carlisle Boarding School Graduates PA.jpg/Wikimedia Commons/Public Domain; p. 49 Barney Hillerman/Underwood Archives/Getty Images; p. 50 United States Department of the Interior/File: Indian Land for Sale.jpg/Wikimedia Commons/Public Domain; p. 50 Photographer Unknown, circa 1870/Burton Historical Collection, Detroit Public Library/File: Bison skull pile-restored.jpg/Wikimedia Commons/Public Domain.

Printed in the United States of America

CONTENTS

INTRODUCTION • 5
Defining the West

CHAPTER ONE • 8
Opening the Frontier

CHAPTER TWO • 21
The Journey West

CHAPTER THREE • 32
The Life of a Homesteader

CHAPTER FOUR • 45
Consequences of Settlement

Chronology • 55

Glossary • 57

Further Information • 59

Bibliography • 60

Index • 62

About the Author • 64

This 1785 map of the United States depicts the area west of the Great Lakes as much smaller than it actually is. This is because the map was created before scientific explorations and surveys of the West were completed.

INTRODUCTION

Defining the West

Over the course of American history, the area defined as the western frontier was not one single place but many different areas. From the beginning of European settlement through well into the nineteenth century, the frontier was a constantly shifting border region at the edge of European (and later American) settlement. In colonial times, that line was the land west of the populated areas on or near the Eastern Seaboard, eventually stretching to the Appalachian Mountains and beyond. After America gained its independence from Britain, the nation's population continued to grow, and the US government began a program of acquisition of western land that would eventually reach the Pacific coast.

In the first half of the nineteenth century, major land acquisitions by the US government—these included the Louisiana Purchase and Mexican Cession territories, which expanded the United States all the way to the Pacific Ocean—opened the entire continent to white settlement.

The first wave of emigrants to the West made the journey by wagon on the major overland trails into the Oregon Territory, California, and Utah, which the Mormons reached before it became US territory. **Homesteading** is defined as acquiring a tract of public land and cultivating and living on it. It was authorized in different forms. Congress passed the Oregon Donation Land Law in 1850, which allowed married homesteaders to claim 320 acres (129 hectares) in that territory.

Later waves of emigrants went west largely due to the Homestead Act, passed during the Civil War in 1862. This law provided a way for (mostly white) individuals and families to achieve the American Dream of land ownership and self-sufficiency. The law started a second wave of westward movement, this time to the Great Plains region, drawing a lot of people into territory that was previously unpopulated. According to the Bureau of Land Management, during the homesteading era more than 1.6 million people staked claims

This 1886 photo shows a family posing next to their prairie schooner wagon in Loup Valley, Nebraska, en route to their new homestead.

to more than 270 million acres (109.3 million hectares). Some of the land claimed, however, had previously been granted to Native Americans.

Homesteading was a difficult life, especially because the best land was granted or sold to the railroad companies and other capitalists who could afford to pay the ticket price. Homesteaders did not own the land outright; they were allowed to settle the land but had to follow certain requirements before they actually owned it. Also, the land was sparsely populated, and there were few towns. Life could be lonely, many families were isolated and left to fend for themselves, and the danger of attack from Native Americans was real.

In 1890, the US Census declared an end to the American frontier. By this time, America had expanded from coast to coast and controlled all the land that makes up the present-day forty-eight contiguous states. America was a major world power, but in achieving this goal, Euro-American settlers wiped out almost the entire population of Native American peoples. They also fought several wars over territory, did devastating damage to the environment and wildlife, and ultimately created an environment where the average American had no chance against wealthy capitalists. For most, the American Dream was still just a dream.

CHAPTER ONE

Opening the Frontier

The late eighteenth to the early nineteenth centuries was a time of great change in the United States. There was massive population growth as well as an influx of European immigrants. The Industrial Revolution was transforming the economy from a farm-based to a manufacturing-based system. As the country expanded, the question of whether or not slavery would be allowed in newly acquired land was a constant source of debate. The slavery question was not the only one driving the settlement of the American West. At the time, it was a widely held belief that white, Protestant Americans were destined by God to settle the continent from coast to coast, spreading Christianity, American civilization, and democratic institutions. There was a common belief that the West was theirs to settle.

Population Growth

The US population growth rate at the turn of the nineteenth century was a driving force behind the settlement of the West.

Charles Volkmar painted *Emigration to America*, which depicts a group of European immigrants arriving in America in the early nineteenth century.

The population of the United States tripled between 1790 and 1830, when there were approximately thirteen million people living in America. Families then were large, and since only one child (usually the firstborn son) could inherit family land, the other children sometimes looked west for land of their own.

There was also a large number of Northern European immigrants coming to America in search of opportunity. Many of these people moved to urban areas, which led to competition for jobs and overcrowding. Others sought to establish their own communities in the West, where they were able to retain their culture and traditions.

Land Boom

There was a land boom in the late eighteenth and early nineteenth centuries that brought many people into the Northwest Territory (present-day Ohio, Indiana, Illinois,

Michigan, Wisconsin, and part of Minnesota). This area was officially created in 1787 by the Northwest Ordinance, which established a system of government and a path to statehood for new territories. Slavery was prohibited in the Northwest Territory and any state created from it. The first permanent white settlement in the Northwest Territory was Marietta, Ohio, which was established in 1788.

An early nineteenth-century engraving shows the courthouse and jail in Marietta, Ohio, which was the first permanent white settlement in the Northwest Territory.

The federal government—at first under the Federalists—encouraged land sales in the territories because the sale of unsettled public land was a form of revenue. The Land Ordinance of 1785 created a method for the sale of public land to private citizens, as well as a system for surveying the land. Land was divided into townships measuring 6 miles by 6 miles (9.6 kilometers), each with thirty-six 1-square-mile sections (640 acres, or 259 hectares, each), which could then be sold to the public at auction (except for one section reserved for public schools). This system, with its price and

Mismanagement of the second Bank of the United States, opened in Philadelphia in 1816, was partly blamed for the Panic of 1819.

acreage too high for most citizens, was designed for groups of settlers from the East to pool resources and form new communities. However, this happened less often than wealthy **land speculators** (a type of real estate entrepreneur) buying up property and then selling it for a profit.

The land purchase system in the early nineteenth century favored the speculator over the farmer. Many farmers took out loans, believing there was little risk since the agriculture-based economy was strong at the time. These small farmers engaged in **cash cropping** (farming a single, marketable crop for profit) so they could repay their loans. This was risky as it relied on a successful harvest, the crop values remaining high, and the success of the banks created to provide credit. Many banks, their depositors, and people with mortgages suffered serious losses in the financial Panic of 1819.

The Louisiana Purchase

In 1803, the single largest land acquisition in American history—the Louisiana Purchase—took place under President

Thomas Jefferson. Jefferson was an early supporter of westward expansion. He believed that the ideal America was a rural, **agrarian** society and that the **yeoman**, or individual landholding farmer, best represented the American values of liberty and equality. To achieve this vision, it was important to acquire new land to cultivate.

The Louisiana Purchase doubled the size of the United States and gave Americans full access to the Mississippi River and the Port of New Orleans, which were both important for trade. This vast new American territory stretched west from the Mississippi River to the Rocky Mountains, and from the Gulf of Mexico in the South to Canada in the North. Jefferson commissioned explorations of this new territory, the first and most famous of which was the Lewis and Clark expedition (1804–1806). The main goal of this and other expeditions was to find the best (ideally water-based) trade routes. It was also important to map and survey the territory, establish an American presence, and to gather information on and establish trade relations with Native American tribes in the territory.

Not everyone supported Jefferson's purchase. The Federalists—the opposition party to Jefferson's Democratic-Republican Party—did not support expansion past the Mississippi River because they believed that extending America's boundaries would weaken the nation and their own political power. They believed that expansion would cause conflict with the colonial governments of Spain in the Southwest and Britain in the Pacific Northwest. Expansion would take the focus off of developing existing territory, as well as make it harder to control and maintain democracy and American (i.e., white Protestant) values throughout the nation.

The Second Great Awakening

The religious movement known as the Second Great Awakening greatly contributed to the push west. This

Protestant religious movement sent its ministers west to spread Christianity to the frontier, which was seen as a lawless and godless place. The Second Great Awakening was based on the concept that the individual Christian could achieve salvation by living a moral life and doing good deeds. It was also based on the belief that it was every Christian's duty to spread the religion across the expanding nation. It was believed that making the country fully Protestant would purify America and bring about the return of Christ, ushering in one thousand years of peace—a belief called **millennialism**. Many ministers and their families moved to the frontier to make sure that Protestant Christianity traveled west with the settlers.

Revival meetings at religious camps brought Protestant Christianity to the newly settled territory on the western frontier.

Changing Economy

The influx of European immigrants in the Northeast during the Industrial Revolution led to an excess of workers, which reduced wages. The working conditions in factories were poor, and the pay was low. As more factories sprang up in the East, there was a shift from an agriculture-based economy to a market economy based on manufactured goods. This required better transportation routes for trade and drove expansion west. Initially, the Mississippi River and the Port of New Orleans were the most important trade routes in the West. However, as time went on, further expansion was driven by the desire for transcontinental trade routes that would give eastern businesses access to trade with Asia via ports on the Pacific coast, as well as expand their domestic markets.

The Missouri Compromise

When proslavery Missouri applied for statehood in 1819, there was an equal amount of slave states and Free States (eleven each). If accepted into the Union, Missouri would throw the congressional balance in favor of the slave states. Missouri's statehood was fiercely debated in Congress, and an agreement called the Missouri Compromise was reached in 1820. This admitted Missouri as a slave state and Maine as a Free State, which maintained the balance. It also established the boundary between slave states and Free States at the 36°30' latitude line. Slavery was banned in all Louisiana Purchase territory north of this line (except Missouri itself). This was a short-term fix for the problem, but it held for the next thirty years.

The Monroe Doctrine

One of the most significant policies of the early nineteenth century was the Monroe Doctrine, without which westward expansion would not have been possible. At this time, parts of what is now the continental United States were still controlled by European powers (Britain and Spain), and Russia claimed areas of Alaska and the Pacific Northwest. During President James Monroe's Seventh Annual Message to Congress on December 2, 1823, he presented a new foreign policy. Monroe stated:

> The occasion has been judged proper for asserting, as a principle in which the rights and interests of the United States are involved, that the American continents, by the free and independent condition which they have assumed and maintain, are henceforth not to be considered as subjects for future colonization by any European power … We owe it, therefore, to candor and to the amicable relations existing between the United States and those powers to declare that we should consider any attempt on their part to extend their system to any portion of this hemisphere as dangerous to our peace and safety.

He added that European interference in independent areas of the Americas would be viewed "as the manifestation of an unfriendly disposition toward the United States."

Britain supported the Monroe Doctrine because it protected its trade interests in the Oregon Territory in the Pacific Northwest. It also protected this territory from claims by Russia and Spain. For the growing United States, the Monroe Doctrine ensured there would be no outside competition for settlement of the West—leaving the indigenous Native Americans as their only competition for land and resources.

Manifest Destiny

In the mid-nineteenth century, the American urge to explore and settle the new land to the west was given a name: **manifest destiny**. This specific term was coined by a

Mexican Texas

One of the first areas outside the Louisiana Purchase territory that was opened for settlement by Euro-Americans would not be part of the United States for years. Present-day Texas was part of the Spanish colony of New Spain until 1821, when Mexicans won their independence from the colonial government. Mexico controlled all of present-day Texas, New Mexico, Arizona, Utah, Nevada, California, and parts of Colorado and Wyoming. This land bordered the western edge of the Louisiana Purchase.

Initially, the Mexican government encouraged trade with the United States and American settlement in Texas. The **empresario** system gave land agents—known as empresarios ("businessman" in Spanish)—large grants of land in Mexican Texas. Empresarios were responsible for bringing American settlers to Texas. In return, they got to keep tracts of land for themselves.

Mexico imposed two rules: slavery was illegal, and the settlers must be Catholic. Settlers ignored these rules. During "Texas Fever" in the 1820s, people from nearby Louisiana, Alabama, and Mississippi moved to Texas. They were mostly Protestant, and many brought slaves. It was common to see "G.T.T." (Gone To Texas) carved into doors of abandoned homes as people left in search of better, cheaper land.

The population of Texians (white American settlers) increased by tens of thousands in just a few years, making the Tejanos (native Mexicans) a minority in their homeland. Soon Texians (and some Tejanos) wanted to secede from Mexico.

After an armed conflict with the Mexican government—the Texas Revolution (1835–1836)—the Republic of Texas declared its independence on

Stephen F. Austin was the second empresario of Mexican Texas.

March 2, 1836. Texas legalized slavery and banned free black settlers. Bringing the Republic of Texas into the Union would cause a shift in the balance of power favoring the proslavery side. This stalled Texas's annexation in Congress for almost a decade.

Opening the Frontier

newspaper columnist named John O'Sullivan in an article he wrote in support of the annexation of Texas in the July–August 1845 issue of *United States Magazine and Democratic Review* (although some historians believe that this unsigned editorial, "Annexation," was actually written by journalist Jane Cazneau). The relevant passage from the editorial reads that bringing Texas into the Union is:

> the fulfillment of our manifest destiny to overspread the continent allotted by Providence for the free development of our yearly multiplying millions.

In O'Sullivan's December 27, 1845, article in the *New York Morning News*, the term was used again, this time in reference to the conflict with Britain over the border of the Oregon Territory:

> Away with all these cobweb issues of rights of discovery, exploration, settlement, continuity, etc. … Our claim to Oregon would still be best and strongest. And that claim is by the right of our manifest destiny to overspread and to possess the whole of the continent which Providence has given us.

The concept of manifest destiny, as described by O'Sullivan and adopted by American politicians of the era, is that white American Protestants have a God-given duty to settle the whole continent, spreading the American ideals of democracy and liberty and bringing "civilization" to the indigenous peoples of the West.

President James K. Polk is the politician most closely associated with manifest destiny. The concept guided his foreign policy decisions, including the annexation of Texas and subsequent war with Mexico, as well as the resolution of

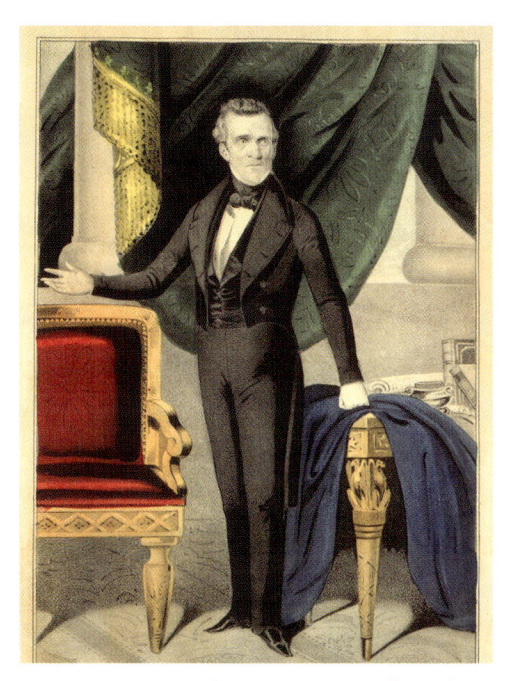

Expansionist president James K. Polk took the United States into war with Mexico.

the border dispute over Oregon. In his inaugural speech on March 4, 1845, Polk addressed the annexation of Texas and described US foreign policy as one of "peace with each other and all the world. To enlarge [the United States'] limits is to extend the dominions of peace over additional territories and increasing millions." He advised foreign powers to "look on the annexation of Texas to the United States not as the conquest of a nation seeking to extend her dominions by arms and violence, but as the peaceful acquisition of a territory once her own."

Polk went on to discuss the settlement of Oregon. The first major wave of emigrants to Oregon Country was already under way, and Polk stated that America's claim to the territory is "clear and unquestionable." He praised the settlers and stated that it is the US government's responsibility to support and protect them in their new land, which he believed was destined to become a part of the Union:

> Already are our people preparing to perfect [Oregon Country] by occupying it with their wives and children … Our people, increasing to many millions, have filled the eastern valley of the Mississippi, adventurously ascended the Missouri to its headsprings, and are already engaged in

Opening the Frontier

> establishing the blessings of self-government in valleys of which the rivers flow to the Pacific ... To us belongs the duty of protecting them adequately wherever they may be upon our soil. The jurisdiction of our laws and the benefits of our republican institutions should be extended over them in the distant regions which they have selected for their homes.

Polk was soon able to resolve the Oregon dispute with Britain. In the Oregon Treaty of 1846, the border was set at the forty-ninth parallel west of the Rocky Mountains (but excluding Vancouver Island). The Texas question was not so easily resolved, in part because Polk was already looking beyond Texas to California.

War with Mexico

When Texas was admitted to the Union as a slave state in 1845, there was a dispute with Mexico over the border. The United States claimed that the Texas territory extended as far south as the Rio Grande River, while Mexico claimed that the border was farther north. Polk wanted to purchase disputed land from Mexico, but his offer was rejected. Fighting broke out when the United States sent troops to the border region, and the US declared war on Mexico on May 13, 1846.

The Treaty of Guadalupe Hidalgo officially ended the Mexican-American War on February 2, 1848. The United States agreed to pay Mexico $15 million in exchange for more than 500,000 square miles (1.3 million sq km) of new territory. This land, called the Mexican Cession, included the present-day states of California, Nevada, and Utah, as well as parts of New Mexico, Arizona, Colorado, and Wyoming. The Mexican Cession was the largest land acquisition since the Louisiana Purchase, and with it the US goal of fully extending it territory from coast to coast was realized.

CHAPTER TWO

The Journey West

As the United States acquired more territory and the government cleared the path for white settlement, several major routes were established for emigrants traveling to new lands. In the 1840s, when the first major wave of emigrants made the journey, the trip was very long and difficult, but the pull of fertile lands and rivers full of gold in the West was hard to resist for many Americans looking for a better life.

Mountain Men

Settlement of the Far West would not have been possible without the first white American settlers—the so-called Mountain Men—who went west shortly after the Lewis and Clark expedition. These men used the available information to make their way to the Rocky Mountains and Oregon Country, where they worked as fur trappers and traders. These men emigrated in the early 1800s, and their explorations are

This 1837 painting by Alfred Jacob Miller depicts the last great rendezvous of fur traders, trappers, and Native Americans near the Green River in Wyoming.

responsible for much of the knowledge later used by settlers on the Oregon Trail—one of the main arteries for the first mass Euro-American migration to the Far West. The fur trade declined because of overhunting and because beaver hats went out of fashion, and many Mountain Men became guides for new emigrants.

As guides, these men were able to help emigrants in their encounters with Native Americans. While working in the fur trade, they formed relationships with Native Americans. There were annual events called **rendezvous** where they would come together with Native American traders and representatives from the fur companies for trading and selling supplies and furs. This was a time when they could restock supplies, but it was also a festival with entertainment, sponsored by the fur companies. At the rendezvous, there was a level of cultural exchange that did not exist outside the fur trading community. Although relations were not universally friendly, the fur traders in the Pacific Northwest had the best relationships with the Native Americans of any European or American settlers in the region.

The Oregon Trail

The first white settlement in Oregon Country started in the 1830s with Protestant missionaries and soon expanded. In 1843, the government sent an engineer, John Charles Frémont, to survey the area of the Oregon Trail. Frémont's survey report was a bestseller that included scientific data and practical information for emigrants: the locations of water sources, land for grazing animals, and other practical tips. This became the main guidebook for early travelers.

In the Great Emigration of 1843, approximately one thousand people made the 2,170-mile (3,492 km) journey from Independence, Missouri, on the Mississippi River to Oregon City in the Willamette Valley. The earliest route took travelers from Missouri through the present-day states of Kansas, Nebraska, Wyoming, Idaho, and Oregon. It followed the Platte River Valley across the Great Plains, to the South Pass through the Rocky Mountains in Wyoming, then followed the Snake River Valley in Idaho to the Cascade Mountains, where travelers had a tough choice between the mountain pass or the Columbia River to reach the Willamette Valley. The journey took four to six months.

Many of the people who went to Oregon in the early years were from the Midwest and were already used to life on the frontier. After the financial Panic of 1837 caused a severe drop in agriculture prices, they moved on in search of more and better land. They were prompted and encouraged by publications that claimed the West was full of fertile land. There was also a literary movement at the time—

William Henry Jackson painted a wagon train of emigrants on the Oregon Trail near the Devil's Gate gorge in Wyoming.

the American School—that popularized the frontier, and emigrants would have been familiar with these works. Author James Fenimore Cooper wrote a series of popular frontier adventure novels, including the famous *Last of the Mohicans* (1826), which romanticized the American pioneer spirit. Another popular frontier novel was *The Adventures of Captain Bonneville* (1837) by Washington Irving.

The California Trail

Some emigrants on the Oregon Trail had a different final destination: California. The gold rush brought many prospectors to the region, and the stories of fertile valleys brought others. Travelers started on the Oregon Trail but headed southwest either in Wyoming or Idaho. The California trails had been known to fur trappers since the early 1800s, but emigrants only really began using them in the 1840s.

California was acquired by the United States as part of the Mexican Cession in February 1848, around the time that gold was discovered there. The first official report of the discovery of gold was from Army Colonel Richard Barnes Mason, who visited John Sutter's mill in Coloma, where gold had been discovered in the American River. His August 1848 report read, in part:

> I have no hesitation now in saying, that there is more gold in the country drained by the Sacramento and San Joaquin Rivers than will pay the cost of the present war with Mexico a hundred times over. No capital is required to obtain this gold, as the labouring man wants nothing but his pick and shovel and tin pan, with which to dig and wash the gravel, and many frequently pick gold out of the crevices of rocks with their knives, in pieces of from one to six ounces [28 to 170 grams].

Accounts of gold being abundant and easy to get drove the mass migration to California in 1849. These first white settlers of California were known as the Forty-Niners.

The Mormon Trail

Mormons were subjected to religious persecution in the nineteenth century, in part because of the practice of plural marriage and also because they tended to settle in large numbers, creating a majority population and competition for jobs and political power. The constant threat of violence pushed the Mormons farther and farther west over the span of just a few years. They were originally driven from Fayette, New York, where Joseph Smith founded the religion in 1830. They then went to Ohio, then Missouri, and finally Nauvoo, Illinois, where they set up a community from 1839 to 1846.

After the murder of founder Joseph Smith in 1844, his successor, Brigham Young, led a mass migration of Mormons

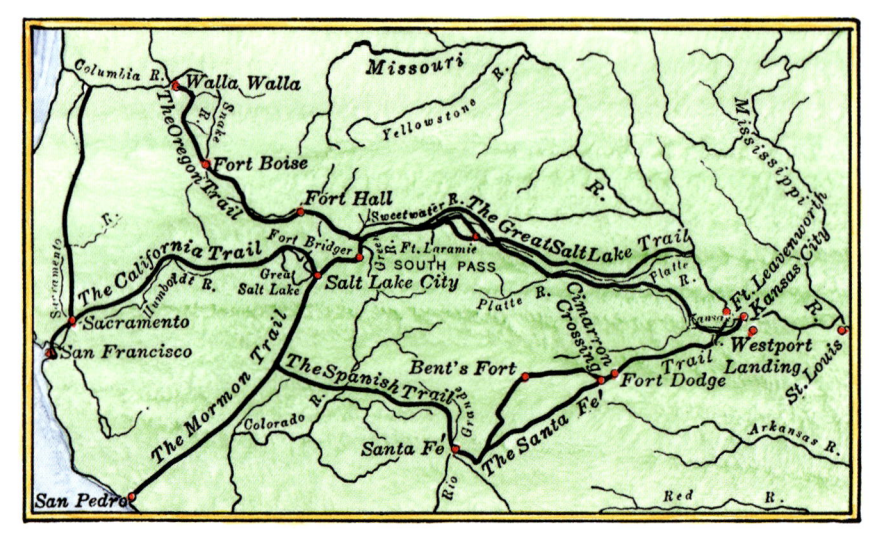

All the major trails in the American West, including the Oregon, California, Mormon, and Santa Fe Trails, are shown in this woodcut.

to Utah Territory, which was still a part of Mexico. The trail stretched from Nauvoo, across the present-day states of Iowa, Nebraska, and Wyoming, and then turned south into the Great Salt Lake valley. The first wave arrived in 1847 and established Salt Lake City. Between 1846 and 1869, approximately seventy thousand Mormons traveled the trail. Many made the journey on foot, pulling handcarts full of their belongings.

Life on the Trail

The earliest emigrants to the West did not have an easy time getting there. Before the railroad was completed, the most common form of transportation was a wagon called the **prairie schooner**. This was smaller than a traditional Conestoga wagon—a heavy wagon used for freight that could not navigate the rougher parts of the trail. Prairie schooners were much lighter and required fewer animals to pull them. They could operate using only one or two horses. This meant there was more food and water per animal over the course of the journey, which went through territory where resources like fresh water and land for grazing were scarce.

In her travel journal, *Reminiscences of a Trip Across the Plains in '45*, pioneer Lucy Jane Hall describes what it was like traveling through the **arid** (dry) territory of the Great Plains on her way to Oregon Country in 1845:

> There was neither grass nor water to be found. All night the men sat by the dim campfires listening for reports from those who had gone in search of water. If any was found a signal of three shots was to be fired in quick succession; if not three shots at intervals. At sunrise no sound had been heard. The train was soon moving on through sagebrush and across dry creek beds which mocked our thirst. So we journeyed till noon, when hark! a shot, but not the three in quick succession, but at intervals; like a death knell they sounded. The men stood in groups talking over the situation, the mothers, pale and haggard, sat in the wagons with their little ones around them. With a determination that knows not defeat the party moved on. About night in quick succession shots were heard, which proclaimed that water had been found. All pushed forward with renewed energy. When in sight of the water the thirsty oxen broke into a run and rushed into the water and drank until they had to be driven out.

Proper provisioning and packing was essential to survive the journey. Families were forced to leave almost everything they owned behind. Every inch of space on the wagon was reserved for essentials. The few available spots to ride in the wagon were reserved for infants, the elderly, and the infirm. Young children and able-bodied men and women would walk alongside the wagon.

The Whitman Massacre

Narcissa Whitman was the first white woman to cross the Rocky Mountains. She left her home in upstate New York in 1836 and traveled the Oregon Trail with her husband, Doctor Marcus Whitman, and a group of other missionaries and fur traders. Theirs was the farthest West of any previous American settlers' expedition. The Whitmans established a Christian mission in Waiilatpu, near present-day Walla Walla, Washington. Like many early Christian settlers, they ministered to the local tribe—the Cayuses.

There was tension between white settlers and the Native people, especially as years went on and the Whitman Mission became a popular stop for white emigrants on the trail. Like other indigenous peoples, the Cayuses had no immunity to European diseases, and when a measles epidemic broke out in 1847, it killed half the tribe. This further strained the relations between whites and Natives, some of whom believed that Dr. Whitman was responsible for the deaths of their people. On November 29, 1847, a group of Cayuses killed the Whitmans and several others. The event became known as the Whitman Massacre and started the eight-year-long Cayuse War with the United States. *The Letters and Journals of Narcissa Whitman* (1836–1847) was published and widely read, contributing to the belief of many white people that all Native Americans were dangerous savages.

William Henry Jackson painted the Whitman Mission circa 1865.

 For the journey, people referenced guidebooks that were published to promote western settlement. Lanford W. Hastings's *The Emigrants' Guide to Oregon and California* (1845) was a popular guide. This detailed and lengthy book provided information about travel to both Oregon and California, detailed descriptions and information about both areas, a description of the routes, and advice regarding equipment, supplies, and method of travel.

 A family of four might pack the following staples: flour, coffee, tea, baking soda, cornmeal, **hardtack** (hard crackers), dried beans, dried fruit, dried beef, molasses, vinegar, salt, pepper, sugar, rice, and lard. Those traveling with livestock like chickens and dairy cows had eggs and fresh milk that enabled

Karl Bodmer painted his travel party, camping overnight on the Missouri River in North Dakota on its way west, in watercolors in 1833.

Homesteading and Settling the Frontier

them to make food. This excerpt from the journal of settler James Meikle Sharp, who crossed the Great Plains with his parents when he was eight years old, demonstrates how butter was made en route:

> The rough roads served us well when it came to the matter of churning the cream for butter. The cream was put in a receptacle and placed in the wagon in the morning. When evening came we were sure to have butter.

The average family of four needed to bring more than 1,000 pounds (454 kilograms) of food to survive the trip. In addition, it needed basic cooking and eating supplies, which were limited to a cast-iron skillet, Dutch oven, **reflector oven**, kettle, tin plates, cups, utensils, matches, and some type of receptacle for liquids (crocks, canteens, buckets, or water bags). Also essential were tools for wagon repairs, as well as basic medical supplies since there was no access to doctors.

All cooking, washing, and sleeping was done outside, subjecting travelers to tough weather conditions for much of the journey. Tents and bedding were basic and did not provide much shelter from the elements. In a letter to her sisters back east, pioneer Narcissa Whitman describes the lack of comfort on the journey:

> Girls, how do you think we manage to rest ourselves every noon, having no house to shelter us from the scorching heat, or sofa on which to recline? Perhaps you think we always encamp in the shade of some thick wood. Such a sight I have not seen, lo, these many weeks. If we can find a few small willows or a single lone tree, we think ourselves amply provided for. But often our camping places are in some open plain and frequently a sand plain.

CHAPTER THREE

The Life of a Homesteader

During the Civil War, when there was no resistance from Southern congressmen, President Abraham Lincoln signed a series of laws that brought the second wave of immigration to the American West. Homesteaders were small farmers from nearby states who wanted better and cheaper land, as well as European immigrants, African Americans fleeing discrimination in the South, and widowed or single women (married women could not claim their own grants). It was a difficult life, but many people found moving to the West a better alternative than conditions in the South and in crowded industrial cities. The arrival of American homesteading families created communities with services, trade, commerce, and government in the new US territories. However, many Native Americans were forced off their homelands to make room for white settlement.

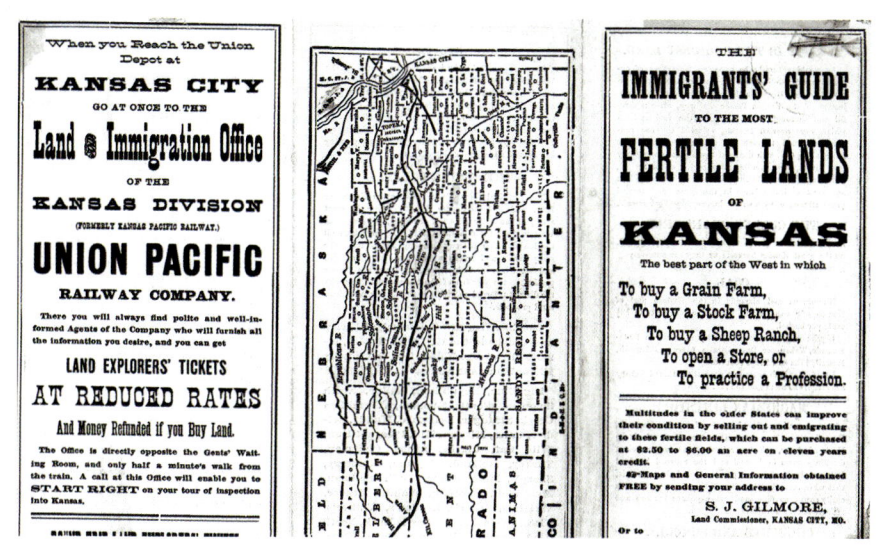

This pamphlet (circa 1880) was circulated to encourage relocation to Kansas. It includes a map of the state and instructions for immigrants.

Settling Kansas

In the years before the Civil War, several laws encouraged the settlement of the West. The Donation Acts of the 1850s encouraged the settlement of the Oregon, Washington, and New Mexico Territories. More important was the Preemption Act of 1841, which allowed **squatters** on federal land to buy it before it became available to the public. These squatters' rights were used during the settlement of Kansas and Nebraska.

The Kansas-Nebraska Act in 1854 opened white settlement of the Kansas and Nebraska Territories and attempted to avoid conflict over the expansion of slavery by instituting **popular sovereignty**. This allowed the settlers of Kansas and Nebraska to decide for themselves whether or not they would allow slavery in their territories. It was thought that Nebraska, next to the Free State of Iowa and the Minnesota Territory, would enter as a Free State, while Kansas, next to the slave state of Missouri, was expected to enter as a slave state, thus keeping the balance in Congress.

However, there was a mad rush by both proslavery and antislavery factions to settle the Kansas Territory so that they could control the territorial government. The factions set up rival governments, and political conflict turned deadly as settlers began to fight. The initial migration led to several years of violent frontier conflict between the settlers. Referred to as "Bleeding Kansas," the conflict was a prelude to the Civil War. The years 1854 through 1859 saw the worst of the violence. The dispute did not really end until 1861, however, when Kansas became a Free State, just months before the beginning of the Civil War.

A photographer captured antislavery settlers in Topeka, Kansas, preparing to fight proslavery forces during the "Bleeding Kansas" period in 1856.

The Homestead Act of 1862

Before the Homestead Act, the federal government used the sale of public land as a source of revenue. Public land was offered in large parcels and at a price the average citizen could not afford or manage. The Homestead Act of 1862, which went into effect January 1, 1863, allowed people to claim 160 acres (65 ha) of land in the Great Plains region, much of which was not yet settled by whites. The act reads, in part, that applicants were required to make an **affidavit** (or statement) confirming that:

> … he or she is the head of a family, or is twenty-one years or more of age, or shall have performed service in the army or navy of the United States, and that he has never borne arms against the Government of the United States or given aid and comfort to its enemies, and that such application is made for his or her exclusive use and benefit, and that said entry is made for the purpose of actual settlement and cultivation.

Under the Homestead Act, the applicant paid a $10 filing fee and would have a recognized but temporary claim on the land. Applicants had six months to start living on and cultivating their land, and after five years they would be the owners if they could prove they met the settlement requirements. If any applicant could meet the requirements after six months, they could buy the land for $1.25 per acre through the act's commutation clause.

The first person to file a claim was Union soldier Daniel Freeman. Freeman filed on January 1, 1863—the first day the law went into effect—and his homestead in Beatrice, Nebraska, was designated a national monument in 1936. After the Civil War ended, the amount of claims increased

This certificate was issued to Daniel Freeman, whose homestead in Beatrice, Nebraska, was the first claimed under the Homestead Act of 1862.

significantly, and by 1872, more than 4.6 million acres (1.86 million ha) had been claimed under the Homestead Act.

Homesteading Fraud

It was the intent of the law that the applicant had to actually live on and improve the land, but there were many unscrupulous people who took advantage of the system to profit off of large tracts of land. Land speculators and railroad companies committed fraud using legal loopholes and bribery of government officials in the General Land Office.

Land speculators took advantage of the Preemption Act and bought up lands before the government had a chance to survey them. They also took advantage of the commutation clause by hiring people to apply for grants and live on the land for six months. The speculators would set up fake homesteads, and at the end of the six-month period, after meeting the most basic requirements, they would buy the land through their fake homesteader who would then sign over the deed.

Some speculators even used portable shacks on wheels that they could move from property to property, as well as fake witnesses to legitimize them. Speculators would then sell the land for profit. These tactics were also used by large companies in the farming, lumber, and cattle industries. The end result was that land speculators and corporations ended up with the best land (the most fertile and/or the closest to the railroad), leaving the average American small farmer to struggle in places where it was much harder to succeed.

Building a Home

One of the requirements for homesteaders was to build a living structure. Because there were few trees on the Great Plains, many houses were built out of **sod** (the top layer of earth that includes grass, dirt, and roots). Homesteaders were also called "sodbusters" because of this building method, and the houses themselves were called "soddies." Cutting sod was a difficult task without mechanized equipment, which the

The Morrison family, on their homestead in Custer County, Nebraska, in 1886, constructed their house out of sod.

average homesteader did not have. The process of building a home took a long time and was hard work that the entire family, including women and children, helped with.

Another type of home was a **dugout**, which was made by digging into a hillside and creating a living space where the floor was a few feet underground. Some homesteaders who could afford to purchase wood built frame houses, but even those required cut sod for insulation and structural support. Building supplies were cheaper and easier to come by after the completion of the transcontinental railroad, but many people still used the earth to build their homes. These types of homes needed constant cleaning—just one of many daily tasks required on the frontier.

It was common for families to settle homesteads neighboring one another to increase the size of the family property. Families would build the necessary structures on the borders of the individual properties, creating a compound, and they would share the domestic and farm labor to make life on the frontier a little bit easier and a little less lonely since there was often no one else around for many miles.

Homesteading Hardships

Many people went west believing in the American Dream of land ownership and self-sufficiency, but many failed to succeed due to the harsh conditions on the frontier. The climate in the Great Plains made traditional methods of farming difficult. People at the time believed that cultivating the land would change the existing climate (which is where the phrase "rain follows the plow" comes from). The plains climate cycles through wet and dry periods, and many people happened to settle the area during a wet period with high rainfall. These wet years (the late 1870s to the early 1880s) were good growth years, and many farmers had initial success, only to suffer when the inevitable dry period followed. Until the mid-1890s, there were severe droughts, heat waves, and high winds that stripped the earth of topsoil exposed for farming and sod construction. The heat, drought, and winds prevented crops from growing and killed livestock.

Access to fresh water was one of the most challenging aspects of homesteading. Many homesteaders' only source of water was collected rainfall, and they had to dig their own wells by hand. Without access to wood for fuel, people had to get creative to heat their homes. One common method of heating the home and cooking was burning **buffalo chips** (dried manure), which had to be collected and hauled to the homestead.

Illness was common because of the unsanitary conditions, including contaminated well water. Doctors and medical supplies were usually far away and expensive. Many homesteaders failed because they didn't have the money for the start-up equipment and supplies, and even those who could afford such expenses had trouble turning a profit from their crops because the trade routes were far away and the market prices were low because of overproduction. The mechanization of farm equipment and the exploitation of the homesteading grants favored large corporate farms, known as **bonanza farms**, which put small farmers at a huge disadvantage. Homesteaders frequently went into debt and ended up abandoning their land.

Women on the Frontier

The first wave of white settlement included many women and families who left behind their established homes and communities. These women had to start over with practically nothing, in places where everyday life was arduous and often dangerous. Women were responsible for all the household tasks, childrearing, and founding community institutions like churches, schools, and social organizations.

Both on the journey west and at the homestead, women were responsible for all food prep, cooking, cleaning, and

Exodusters

The first wave of African American emigrants began in the late 1870s, after the end of Reconstruction brought increased violence and discriminatory Jim Crow laws to the South. These emigrants were called "Exodusters," and they settled mainly in Kansas, Oklahoma, and Texas. One of the leaders of this migration was a former slave named Benjamin "Pap" Singleton, who became known as the "Father of the Exodus." Singleton believed that farm ownership was crucial to the success of African Americans, who were unable to prosper in the post-Reconstruction South. Singleton and his partner, Columbus M. Johnson, started a company called the Edgefield Real Estate and Homestead Association to help African Americans settle in Kansas. Singleton used posters circulated in African American communities to urge people to go west. Between 1877 and 1879, Singleton brought more than twenty thousand black settlers to Kansas.

One of the earliest black homesteading towns was Nicodemus, Kansas, which was founded in 1877 on the Solomon River. Like other homesteaders, they faced harsh conditions, but Nicodemus was a strong community that persevered, and by 1880 the town had grown to almost five hundred people. It included a post office, a bank, a school, churches, hotels, and stores, and it had its own newspaper. By 1887, it had even more businesses, as well as legal services, charity groups, a baseball team, a literary society, and an ice cream parlor. At one point Nicodemus had hopes of access to the railroad, but the route did not end up near the town, and Nicodemus went into decline.

The second wave of African American westward migration occurred in the early twentieth century, after

African American settlers, known as Exodusters, pose in front of their house in Nicodemus, Kansas.

the passage of the 1909 Enlarged Homestead Act. This offered people more land (320 acres, or 130 ha), but it was in undesirable areas with poor conditions. Some of the black homesteaders went west to Colorado and established communities such as "The Dry" in the southern part of the state and Dearfield in the north.

The Life of a Homesteader

gathering fuel (usually hay or manure). They had to make everything completely from scratch with very little equipment and in poor conditions. Cleaning and laundry without good access to water was also very difficult. Women also faced dangers that men did not. Pregnancy and childbirth were very dangerous. Women died without access to doctors or modern medical knowledge. Women also had many more children in those days, which put a strain on their health. On the frontier, there was always the danger of losing a child during birth, and afterward to illness or accidents.

Women had many responsibilities on the homestead as well. They were responsible for tending the family garden, a main source of food. They also tended livestock like chickens,

Laura Ingalls Wilder

Laura Ingalls Wilder, author of the famous "Little House" series of children's books, grew up in a homesteading family. The Ingalls family moved a lot, taking advantage of the Homestead Act. From her birthplace in Wisconsin, the family moved to Independence, Kansas. Like many homesteaders, the Ingalls family settled on land that belonged to Native Americans (in this case, the Osages). Fearing an army sweep of the illegal homesteads in the region, the family moved briefly back to Wisconsin and then on to Walnut Grove, Minnesota, where they originally lived in a dugout home. After a brief time spent in Iowa, the family moved to a homestead in De Smet, South Dakota, where Laura spent her adolescence and early adult life. Many of the "Little House" books are set in De Smet and are fictionalized accounts of Laura's own experiences on the frontier.

A female homesteader gathers hay on a homestead on the Plains. Hay was used for fuel in areas where there were no trees.

pigs, and dairy cows, and many also worked in the fields or on the ranches if the family needed additional help. Out of necessity, women on the frontier often did things considered "men's work."

In areas with more developed communities, some women worked outside the home as well. They were teachers, medical professionals, business owners, domestic servants, clothes washers, seamstresses, and midwives, among other things. Women were also in charge of community building through volunteer work, which included fundraising for the establishment of schools, churches, hospitals, and libraries.

The nature of life on the frontier made gender roles in the West different from those in the East, and as a result, there was a lot of female activism. Western women were involved in national movements such as women's suffrage and the temperance movement against alcohol. White women in the West were allowed to vote as early as 1900 in the states of

Wyoming, Utah, Colorado, and Idaho—twenty years before the Nineteenth Amendment enfranchised all white women. (Black women continued to struggle for voting equality well into the 1960s.)

Since the Homestead Act allowed single women to file their own claims, the West was a place where women could achieve independence. Elinore Pruitt Stewart, a widow with a young child, moved to Wyoming in 1909 and filed a homestead claim. She wrote about her experiences in letters to a friend that were published in *Atlantic Monthly* magazine and later as *Letters of a Woman Homesteader*. Here Stewart describes the independence that homesteading provided for industrious women:

> To me, homesteading is the solution of all poverty's problems, but I realize that temperament has much to do with success in any undertaking, and persons afraid of coyotes and work and loneliness had better let ranching alone. At the same time, any woman who can stand her own company, can see the beauty of the sunset, loves growing things, and is willing to put in as much time at careful labor as she does over the washtub, will certainly succeed; will have independence, plenty to eat all the time, and a home of her own in the end.

CHAPTER FOUR

Consequences of Settlement

The rapid expansion of the United States in the nineteenth century changed the face of the nation in several ways. The opening of the West allowed for the completion of the transcontinental railroad that transformed the US economy. The power of the federal government expanded with the acquisition of new territory. The settlement of new regions forced settlers to adapt and brought about technological innovation, but it also changed the environment, sometimes to disastrous effect. But of all the consequences of expansion, the most devastating was the Native American genocide and the forced removal of the surviving Native peoples onto government reservations.

Indian Removal

The idea that white Protestant Americans were uniquely qualified to "civilize" other (nonwhite) cultures was used as a rationalization for the US government's American Indian removal and assimilation policies throughout the nineteenth century. The idea was not a new one; proslavery factions had been arguing the same thing for years as a way to rationalize the continued existence of slavery in an America built on the concept that all men are created equal. However, this founding principle did not apply to nonwhite citizens, and in the context of westward expansion, this was especially true of Native American tribes. White Americans, especially politicians, pushed the idea that indigenous peoples were savages who needed to be civilized. However, this was just a means to turn popular opinion against them and rationalize aggressive removal policies.

In 1829, Andrew Jackson became the first western president. He was from the old frontier state of Kentucky, and in his military career he had fought and killed many Native Americans. Jackson signed the Indian Removal Act of 1830, which gave the president the power to negotiate removal treaties with Native Americans living east of the Mississippi River and grant them unsettled lands in the West. This land, in the Great Plains region, was arid, unlike their fertile eastern homelands. Some tribes went voluntarily, but many were pressured into signing treaties. Many resisted, and throughout the nineteenth century, the United States government was consistently at war with Native American tribes who refused to go without a fight.

The Indian Appropriations Act of 1851 cleared the way for further white settlement of the West. It created the **reservation system**, which set defined areas for tribes in designated Indian Territory (mostly present-day Oklahoma). The US government promised to provide protection as well as money, food, livestock, and farming equipment, but they often did not meet these obligations. There were also many corrupt agents in the Bureau of Indian Affairs.

The reservation system was used as a means to assimilate Native Americans into white Christian society and strip them of their tribal identities. The US government operated

Native American graduates of Carlisle Indian Industrial School in Pennsylvania sat for a photograph in the 1890s.

boarding schools and required all Native children to attend. Children were taken away from their parents and tribal elders—the keepers of Native culture, language, and traditions—and forced to conform to white Christian standards of dress, language, and worship. They were not even allowed to keep their own names.

The Homestead Act opened up even more Indian Territory for white settlement, which led to land rushes in parts of Oklahoma and the Dakotas in the late nineteenth century. Many of the tribes in these areas had already been relocated from eastern homelands in the early nineteenth century, and there was constant warfare between tribes in all regions of settlement against the white settlers and US Army forces. Homesteading rights were eventually opened up to

Native Americans, but individuals could only participate if they abandoned their tribe and assimilated into white society.

The Indian Appropriations Act of 1871 stripped tribes of their status as independent nations, and the Dawes Act of 1887 (also known as the General Allotment Act) took things even further:

> In all cases where any tribe or band of Indians has been, or shall hereafter be, located upon any reservation created for their use, either by treaty stipulation or by virtue of an act of Congress or executive order setting apart the same for their use, the President of the United States be, and he hereby is, authorized, whenever in his opinion any reservation or any part thereof of such Indians is advantageous for agricultural and grazing purposes, to cause said reservation, or any part thereof, to be surveyed, or resurveyed if necessary, and to allot the lands in said reservation in severalty to any Indian located thereon.

The US government divided former tribal lands into 160-acre (65 ha) parcels and made them available to individual Native Americans. However, instead of the same five-year plan given to other homesteaders, Native Americans could not own the land for twenty-five years. Until then, it belonged to the US government. These laws stripped Native Americans of the power of tribal unity. Those who did not die from war or disease lost their land and their cultural identities.

With no other means to resist settlement of their lands, some tribes went to war. After the Civil War, the United States military was mostly focused on fighting Native American tribes, and most of the army was in the West. The Indian Wars period lasted through the late nineteenth

The Oklahoma Land Rush, the first rush to claim unassigned lands belonging to Native Americans, started at high noon on April 22, 1889.

century, culminating with the massacre of the Sioux at Wounded Knee, South Dakota, in 1890.

Completion of the Transcontinental Railroad

The main US goal in fulfilling its manifest destiny by expanding its territory to the Pacific was the construction of the transcontinental railroad. This opened new domestic trade routes and international trade with Asia. It also shortened the journey west, which encouraged more settlement as well as leisure travel. For the first time, it was possible for people in the East to vacation in the West or to visit family.

When the transcontinental railroad was completed in 1869, travel from New York to San Francisco took eight days, where before it had been a six-month journey. The price of a train ticket was far less than that of an extended wagon trip. Railroad companies promoted settlement—and use of their trains—through advertisements and brochures meant to attract settlers, especially immigrants, to the West.

The states themselves also encouraged settlement by European immigrants. California, Montana, Washington, Oregon, New Mexico, and Colorado all published materials describing in great detail what they had to offer prospective residents. The existence of the railroad and the encouragement from states in the Far West caused many immigrants to bypass the eastern cities after entering through Ellis Island and head west to establish their own communities—cultural enclaves where they could maintain aspects of their culture and traditions.

A 1911 ad from the Department of the Interior promotes the sale of Native lands.

Environmental Damage

The settlement of the West opened the land itself to exploitation by extraction industries like mining, fishing, logging, ranching, and farming. These industries stripped the land of its natural resources and caused pollution. This was especially true in the Great Plains, where farming practices caused the destruction of natural grasslands and soil erosion. Industrial mining polluted water sources. Overgrazing and deforestation caused the loss of habitat for local fauna as well as a change in the soil and climate in regions stripped of trees. When the trees were gone, there was nothing to shield the soil from the heat of the sun or keep any water in the soil. This affected both soil quality and the water cycle, which in turn

Bison Butchering

Before westward expansion, the number of bison—often mistakenly called buffalo—in the United States was estimated to be at least thirty million. By the end of the nineteenth century, they were nearly extinct. Several factors led to the endangerment of the bison. One of the tactics of the US Indian removal policy was to destroy their resources. Since the Plains Indians relied on bison as their main source of food and hides, the government targeted the bison population for extinction to drive the Native peoples off the Great Plains and open the territory for white settlement. The settlers who moved in and started cultivating the land destroyed the bison's natural grassland habitat. The expansion of the railroad changed the animals' migration patterns.

Bison hides were in high demand for making leather, and rail access enabled better trade access. Whereas the Native Americans who relied on the bison did not waste a single part of the animal and thus did not overhunt them, many for-profit hunters only wanted the hide and left the rest to rot. This was also true of sport hunters, who were able to travel to bison country on the railroad and easily hunt them with guns.

This mid-1870s photo shows a man standing on a pile of bison skulls.

Consequences of Settlement

changed the climate of the region. Overfishing and hunting brought many species to the brink of extinction, but none so quickly and aggressively as the bison.

Technological Advancements

The mechanization of farm equipment during the nineteenth-century expansion included the steel plow and the mechanical reaper, which allowed more land to be covered by fewer workers. This was good for large-scale operations but not so much for the independent farmer.

In the Great Plains, where water was scarce, people used windmills to pump groundwater from wells. The Halladay windmill with steel blades was invented in 1854 and remains a common sight in the fields of the Great Plains and the Midwest. The lack of timber made it hard for homesteaders to fence off land with no natural boundaries. Barbed wire was invented in 1867 as a cheap steel alternative to wood or stone fencing. Wire fences helped settlers keep their livestock in, protect crops from ranging livestock, and designate the borders of their property. They were widely used in the West.

The refrigerated rail car was one of the most significant inventions of the period. It made it possible to ship perishable goods across the country, including produce, dairy, and especially meat. No longer did ranchers have to drive and ship live animals via railroad to get beef to the market in the East.

Because many settlers lived in remote areas without access to stores, mail-order catalogs became a popular way to buy manufactured goods at reasonable prices. The popularity of mail-order catalogs like Montgomery Ward and Sears and Roebuck was due to the fact that purchasing manufactured goods saved frontier women the time and energy it took to make all the clothing from scratch. Other popular items in the catalogs were furniture and hardware.

The telegraph was the most important development in long-distance communication in the early nineteenth century.

Many homesteaders used mail order catalogs like this Sears, Roebuck & Co. Consumer's Guide from 1900 to purchase basic supplies in rural areas where there was no access to consumer goods.

Consequences of Settlement

Developed by Samuel Morse in the 1830s and 1840s, the electric telegraph was an easy, fast alternative to handwritten letters, which could take many weeks to deliver between distant locations across the country. The telegraph used wires and electricity to transmit messages quickly. Operators used Morse code—in which each number and letter of the alphabet was assigned its own signal—to transmit the messages. The transcontinental telegraph was completed in 1861. The entire constitution of Nevada was sent by telegraph to Washington, DC, on October 26, 1864. Its swift arrival allowed Nevada to be admitted to the Union before the election, and the new state's votes helped reelect Abraham Lincoln.

Expansion of Federal Power

From the very beginning, the federal government encouraged westward expansion. As the US acquired more territory, the power and influence of the federal government grew. The government controlled the territories before they were accepted into the Union as states. Native American policy was determined and carried out by the federal government via the US military, and most military personnel were stationed in the West after the Civil War. There was a huge federal presence in the life of westerners. There were many army posts and personnel protecting white settlers from what they believed was the ever-present threat of attack by Native Americans.

The federal government also controlled all the land that would become the transcontinental railroad and decided its route. The government appointed all major positions within territorial governments as well as federal employees such as postal service workers, land agents, army engineers, US marshals, Indian agents, and customs agents. The federal government now owns and operates more than 630 million acres (255 million ha) of land in the West, a lot of which is designated as public land or national parkland.

Chronology

Dates in green pertain to events discussed in this volume.

May 20, 1785: Land Ordinance of 1785 is passed, creating a system of surveying new territory acquired by the United States.

July 13, 1787: Northwest Ordinance is passed, creating the Northwest Territory and establishing a system of government and a path to statehood for territories.

October 20, 1803: US Senate ratifies the Louisiana Purchase, which doubles the size of the United States, giving white settlers full access to the Mississippi River and Port of New Orleans trade routes.

August 24, 1821: Mexico wins its independence from the Spanish colonial government.

May 28, 1830: President Andrew Jackson signs the Indian Removal Act. This act gives the president the power to negotiate removal treaties with Native Americans living east of the Mississippi River.

May 25, 1836: Protestant missionaries Marcus and Narcissa Whitman join a wagon train to travel to Oregon Country. They open a mission near present-day Walla Walla, Washington.

March 2, 1836: Republic of Texas wins independence from Mexico.

September 4, 1841: Preemption Act, granting squatters' rights to settlers living on land not yet surveyed by the US government, is passed.

1843: John Charles Frémont surveys what will become the Oregon Trail; the first mass migrations of settlers travels to Oregon Country via the Oregon Trail. The provisional government of Oregon allows homesteading couples to claim 640 acres (259 ha).

March 1, 1845: United States Congress ratifies the treaty to annex Texas.

June 15, 1846: US treaty with Britain finalizes borders of Oregon Territory.

February 10, 1846: First mass migration of Mormons leaves Nauvoo, Illinois to begin journey to the Great Salt Lake Valley in Utah. The journey ends July 24, 1847.

January 24, 1848: Gold is discovered near Coloma, California. Confirmation of the find by President James K. Polk

Chronology 55

in December 1848 kicks off a mass migration to California in 1849.

February 2, 1848: Treaty of Guadalupe-Hidalgo, which ends the Mexican-American War, is signed in Mexico. It also grants to the United States the Mexican Cession territory.

September 9, 1850: California enters the Union as a free state.

September 27, 1850: Donation Land Claim Act is passed to encourage homesteading in Oregon Territory.

February 27, 1851: Indian Appropriations Act passes, creating the reservation system and clearing the way for further white settlement.

May 30, 1854: The Kansas-Nebraska Act creates the territories of Kansas and Nebraska, setting off a civil war in Kansas between proslavery and antislavery settlers.

May 20, 1862: Homestead Act passes. It grants 160 acres (65 ha) of land to settlers who meet residency and improvement requirements.

March 3, 1873: Timber Culture Act is signed by President Ulysses S. Grant. It allows homesteaders to gain an additional 160 acres (65 ha) of land if they plant trees on a certain percentage of landholdings.

April 18, 1877: African American "Exodusters" settle the town of Nicodemus, Kansas.

April 2, 1889: Approximately fifty thousand people, known as Boomers, race into what is now central Oklahoma to stake land claims on 2 million acres (809,371 ha) of Indian Territory opened to homesteaders.

June 2, 1890: US Census starts, with findings showing the end of the American frontier.

Glossary

affidavit A sworn statement in writing made especially under oath.

agrarian Of or relating to farming or the cultivation of land.

arid A dry climate having insufficient rainfall to support agriculture.

bonanza farms Corporate farms with large-scale production operations and easy access to shipping routes.

buffalo chips Dried manure used for fuel in areas without access to wood.

cash crop A crop produced for sale and profit rather than for use by the farmer.

dugout Form of shelter dug into a hillside by homesteaders in areas where wood was not available for construction.

empresario A person who entered into a contract with the Spanish or Mexican government to settle people in Texas in exchange for large land grants.

hardtack Hard dry bread or biscuits.

homesteading The act of acquiring a tract of public land (often 160 acres, or 65 hecatres) from the US government by filing a record and living on and cultivating the land.

land speculator A person who purchased large amounts of land in the West for resale later at a higher price.

manifest destiny The belief that the expansion of the United States throughout the American continents was both justified and divinely ordained.

millennialism The belief that spreading Protestant Christianity throughout America would purify the nation and bring about the return of Christ and one thousand years of peace.

popular sovereignty A principle that allowed the people living in a territory to determine their own laws, especially with respect to slavery.

prairie schooner A covered wagon used by nineteenth-century pioneers to cross the North American prairies.

reflector oven A metal container, usually tin, designed to cook food by enclosing it on all but one side, capturing heat from an open fire, and reflecting the heat toward the food.

rendezvous A meeting held once per year in the wilderness that included a major transfer of furs and goods.

reservation system A US government system that established boundaries for the territory of each Native American tribe.

sod The top layer of earth that includes grass, dirt, and roots.

squatter A pioneer who settled and improved lands before they had been surveyed by the United States government.

yeoman A person who owns and cultivates a small farm.

Further Information

Books

Musolf, Neil. *The Split History of Westward Expansion in the United States.* North Mankato, MN: Compass Point Books, 2012.

Peavy, Linda, and Ursula Smith. *Pioneer Women: The Lives of Women on the Frontier.* Norman, OK: University of Oklahoma Press, 1996.

Roza, Greg. *Westward Expansion.* Story of America. New York: Gareth Stevens Publishing, 2011.

Wade, Mary Dodson. *Homesteading on the Plains.* Minneapolis, MN: Millbrook Press, 1997.

Websites

Diaries, Memoirs, Letters, and Reports Along the Trails West
http://www.over-land.com/diaries.html
A large collection of primary-source writings by explorers and homesteaders who made the trek west.

Digital History: Pre–Civil War Era
http://www.digitalhistory.uh.edu/era.cfm?eraID=5&smtid=2
Online resource providing historical context for westward expansion, primary-source documents related to the era, and articles on pioneers and life on the trails.

PBS: Frontier Life
http://www.pbs.org/wnet/frontierhouse/frontierlife/index.html
Excellent resource for information on settling the frontier. Includes many primary sources, including diary entries, photographs, newspaper articles, and government documents.

Bibliography

Books

Butler, Anne M., and Michael J. Lansing. *The American West: A Concise History*. Malden, MA: Blackwell Publishing, 2008.

Greenberg, Amy S., ed. *Manifest Destiny and Territorial Expansion: A Brief History with Documents*. Boston: Bedford/St. Martin's, 2012.

Hine, Robert V., and John Mack Faragher. *The American West: A New Interpretive History*. New Haven, CT: Yale University Press, 2000.

Milner, Clyde A., II, Carol A. O'Connor, and Martha A. Sandweiss, eds. *The Oxford History of the American West*. New York: Oxford University Press, 1994.

Moulton, Candy. *The Writer's Guide to Everyday Life in the Wild West from 1840–1900*. Cincinnati, OH: Writer's Digest Books, 1999.

Peavy, Linda, and Ursula Smith. *Pioneer Women: The Lives of Women on the Frontier*. Norman, OK: University of Oklahoma Press, 1996.

Quay, Sara E. *Westward Expansion*. Westport, CT: Greenwood Press, 2002.

Wade, Mary Dodson. *Homesteading on the Plains*. Minneapolis, MN: Millbrook Press, 1997.

Online Articles

Hall, Lucy Jane. "Reminiscences of a Trip Across the Plains in '45." Oregon Pioneer Biographies. Accessed November 24, 2016. http://www.rootsweb.ancestry.com/~orgenweb/bios/plains.html.

Whitman, Narcissa. "The Letters and Journals of Narcissa Whitman, 1836–1847." Archives of the West. Accessed November 24, 2016. http://www.pbs.org/weta/thewest/resources/archives/two/whitman1.htm.

Wrenn, Sara B., and Mrs. J. R. Bean. "Overland Trail Lore and Early Life," January 31, 1939. US Work Projects Administration, Federal Writers' Project. https://www.loc.gov/item/wpalh001963.

Index

Page numbers in **boldface** are illustrations. Entries in **boldface** are glossary terms.

affidavit, 35
agrarian, 12
arid, 27, 46

bison, 51–52
Bleeding Kansas, 34, **34**
bonanza farms, 39
buffalo chips, 39

cash crop, 11
Civil War, 6, 32–35, 48, 54

Donation Acts, 6, 33
dugout, 38, 42

empresario, 16
Exodusters, 40, **41**

Frémont, John C., 23
fur trade, 21–24, 28

gold rush, 24–25
guidebooks, 23, 29

hardtack, 29
Homestead Act, 6, 35–37, 42, 44, 47

homesteading, 6–7, 32, 35–44, **37**, **41**, **43**, 47–48, 52

Indian Removal Act, 46
Industrial Revolution, 8, 14

Jackson, Andrew, 46
Jefferson, Thomas, 11–12

Kansas-Nebraska Act, 33–34

land speculator, 11, 36–37
Lewis and Clark expedition, 12, 21
Lincoln, Abraham, 32, 54
literature, 23–24, 42
Louisiana Purchase, 5, 11–12, 14, 16, 20

mail-order catalogs, 52, **53**
manifest destiny, 8
mechanized farm equipment, 39, 52
medicine, 31, 39, 42–43
Mexican-American War, 18, 20, 25
Mexican Cession, 5, 20, 24
millennialism, 13
Missouri Compromise, 14
Monroe Doctrine, 14–15
Mormons, 6, 25–26

62 Homesteading and Settling the Frontier

Nicodemus, Kansas, 40, **41**
Northwest Ordinance, 9–10

Oregon Trail, 6, 21–24, **24**, **26**, 28–29

Polk, James K., 18–20, **19**
popular sovereignty, 33–34
prairie schooner, **6**, 26
Preemption Act, 33, 36

railroads, 7, 26, 36–38, 40, 45, 49–52, 54
reflector oven, 31
rendezvous, 22–23, **22**
reservation system, 45–48

Second Great Awakening, 12–13, **13**
settlement of the frontier
  African Americans and, 32, 40–41, **41**
  daily life, 7, 32, 37–40, 37, 42–44
  early settlement, 9–11, 16, 21–23
  economics and, 7, 10–11, 36–37, 39
  environmental impact, 7, 45, 50–52

legislation promoting, 6, 32–33, 35–37, 41, 44, 47–48
migration process, **6**, 21, 23–27, **24**, **26**, 29, **30**, 31, 49–50
Native Americans and, 7, 28, 32, 42, 45–49, 50
religion and, 12–13, 23, 25–26, 28
statistics, 6–7, 23, 26, 40
women and, 28, 32, 39, 42–44, **43**
Singleton, Benjamin, 40
slavery, 8, 10, 14, 16–17, 20, 33–34, 40, 46
sod, 37–39, **37**
squatter, 33

telegraph, 52, 54
Texas, 16–20, 40

Whitman Mission, 28, **29**
Wilder, Laura Ingalls, 42
women's suffrage, 43–44
Wounded Knee Massacre, 49

yeoman, 12

About the Author

ALISON MORRETTA holds a bachelor of arts in English and creative writing from Kenyon College in Gambier, Ohio, where she studied literature and American history. She has written many nonfiction titles for middle and high school students on subjects such as American literature, the abolitionist movement, the civil rights era, and Islamophobia. She lives in New York City with her loving husband, Bart, and their rambunctious Corgi, Cassidy.